Riddles of the Stars

Other books by Robert Kraske

The Sea Robbers

Is There Life in Outer Space?

The Story of the Dictionary

Robert Kraske

Illustrated with photographs

Riddles of the Stars

White Dwarfs,
Red Giants,
and
Black Holes

Harcourt Brace Jovanovich / New York and London

Copyright © 1979 by Robert Kraske

Printed in the United States of America

Library of Congress Cataloging in Publication Data

Kraske, Robert.
Riddles of the stars.

Includes index.
SUMMARY: Discusses the birth, death, and characteristics
of stars and what has been learned from studying them.
    1. Stars—Juvenile literature.   [1. Stars]
I. Title.
QB801.7.K72   523.8   79-87520
ISBN 0-15-266907-8

First edition

B C D E F G H I J K

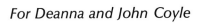

For Deanna and John Coyle

Contents

One

The Sun:
Our Lucky Star

Here is a riddle. How are stars and people alike?

Answer: Like people, stars are born, live for many years, and then die.

Most people live for sixty or seventy years. Stars live for millions—even billions—of years. But sooner or later they wink out. Floating in space are thousands and millions of dead stars, cold and dark. We can't see them in the night sky. Astronomers can't see them through powerful telescopes. But we know these dead stars are out there.

How do scientists know that stars die? It's easy to know this about people. We can study people close up. But stars are not so easy to study. They are far away, out in space. How can we know so much about them?

There was a time, about 150 years ago, when scientists believed that we could never learn anything about the stars. One Frenchman, Auguste Comte, longed to know what the stars were made of. But it was impossible, he said, to study objects so far away. "There are some things of which the human race must remain forever in ignorance."

Today, however, astronomers have special instruments to study the stars. Right here on earth, they say, we can tell what a star blinking far out in space is made of. We can tell just as if we had a chunk of that star under a microscope.

Amazing scientific instruments have helped us learn about the stars, yes, but there is another reason we know so much about them. We have our own star to study. We call it the sun, but we really should call it the star. Our sun is a star just like all the other pinpoints of light twinkling in the night sky. (We see stars twinkling because their light passes through moving layers of air around the earth before it reaches our eyes. Astronauts in spaceships above earth's blanket of air, however, see stars shining as steady points of light.)

Over the years since Auguste Comte made his gloomy statement, scientists have learned many things about the stars. The *number* of stars, for example. On a clear night, we can see 2,000 to 4,000. If we look through a telescope with a 3-inch lens, we can see 600,000. The largest telescope in the United States—the great Hale telescope in California—can see 3 *billion*.

Yet this is hardly a handful of the stars in the sky. Astronomers guess that, in the universe—in all space beyond earth—there are about 200 billion billion stars. This number is so big that it is almost without meaning. Written out, it looks like this:

$$200,000,000,000,000,000,000,000$$

So many stars. Even *1* billion is hard to think of. If you counted one star each second for eight hours each night, it would take ninety-five years to count 1 billion stars.

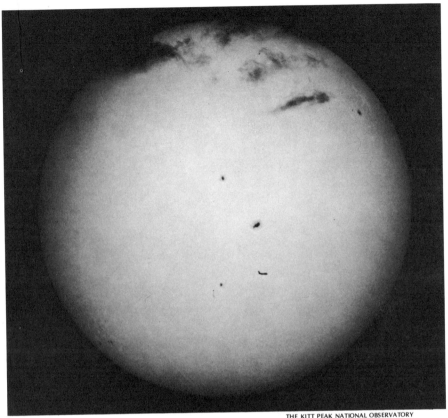

The rising sun. A telescope 50 miles from Tucson, Arizona, took this photograph. The dark object in the lower right is an airplane. It was over Texas when the picture was taken. The sun is 93,000,000 miles out in space.

When we look at stars in the night sky, they appear close together. They look close together because some stars are behind others, but we see them all at once. Yet stars are really very far apart. An astronomer might describe the distance between stars like this:

Think about your school gym or auditorium. Big, empty rooms, aren't they? Imagine two flies buzzing

THE KITT PEAK NATIONAL OBSERVATORY

The McMath solar telescope. World's largest sun telescope is at Kitt Peak National Observatory in Arizona. At the top of the tower, an 80-inch-wide mirror follows the sun across the sky. This mirror reflects the sun down a 500-foot tunnel, at right, 300 feet of which is underground. A 60-inch mirror at the bottom reflects the sun's image back up the tunnel to a 48-inch mirror. This third mirror then reflects the image to an observation room. There scientists study the sun's image on a flat "table." The McMath telescope can "see" features on the sun that are about 400 miles wide, about the size of the state of Minnesota.

14

Sun on a table. The McMath Solar Telescope stands on land belonging to the Papago Indians. Here three Indian girls on a visit from school examine the sun's image on the "table" in the observation room. Each year, many schools send students to see this telescope.

around in those empty spaces. What chance is there that they might bump into each other? Very little. It's the same way out in space. Most stars float around in space with as much room around them as a single fly in a huge auditorium.

It's hard to imagine just how far away from our star the nearest star is. Let's say, though, that our star is the size of a grapefruit. If our grapefruit star were in New York City, the nearest star would be another grapefruit in Los Angeles, California. Look at a map of the United States. You will see how far from our "grapefruit" the next closest "grapefruit" is.

In space, the star closest to our star is Alpha Centauri. It is about 26 trillion miles away. From Alpha Centauri, our star would look like a bright gold "o" in this sentence. Earth—our little planet on which so many people live in so many countries—would not even be visible.

Where do stars go in the daytime? Nowhere. They stay right where they are—only we can't see them. Our star shines so brightly that we can't see other stars shining during the day.

Stars shine day and night and give off heat and light just as our star does. If they were as close to earth as our sun, they would give us a sunburn and cast shadows around us on the ground.

Stars come in all sizes. The smallest stars astronomers know about are smaller than earth. One star, called Van Maanen's Star, is 5,200 miles in diameter, the distance through the center. Earth is almost 8,000 miles in diameter. Astronomers call Van Maanen's Star a dwarf star. But it is not the smallest star in the heavens. Some stars are even smaller.

Our star is average in size. About half of all stars in the universe are larger than our star; about half are

Earth in space. American astronauts on a space flight to the moon took this picture. It shows earth in the blackness of space. The white area at the bottom is the ice cap at the South Pole. The earth is 7,926 miles wide. The sun is 864,000 miles wide—109 times wider than earth.

smaller. Yet when compared to earth, our star is big—865,000 miles through the center. Compared to the sun, earth is like a golf ball on a round rug 15 feet wide.

For another idea of the sun's size, try this:

Some night look at the moon. The moon is about 238,000 miles away. It moves around earth in a near circle, or orbit, 476,000 miles wide. Imagine our sun sliced in half, like an orange sliced in two. One of these halves would just about hold the earth and the moon in its orbit.

Here's a way to picture the mass of our sun—the amount of material it contains. Let's say that the sun and all nine planets in orbit around it—Mercury, Venus, earth, Mars, Jupiter, Saturn, Uranus, Neptune, and Pluto—weighed as much as 1,000 bricks. Look at the bricks in a large brick wall—maybe in one wall of your school. Count 1,000. Our star would weigh as much as 999 bricks; *all* the planets, only as much as *one* brick!

Our star seems big to us, but in the universe there are stars so big that they make our star look like a Ping-Pong ball. Astronomers call them supergiants. Two supergiants that we can see without telescopes are Antares and Betelgeuse. Antares is 330 times wider than our sun. Betelgeuse is about 350 times wider.

In 1921 scientists managed to measure Betelgeuse. It was 300 million miles wide.

Amazed that anything could be this big, a science writer tried to describe Betelgeuse for his readers. Think of a fourteen-year-old boy standing on Betelgeuse, he wrote. The boy has just shot a rifle. Each second the bullet will travel 2,800 feet. Each hour it will cover nearly 2,000 miles. But Betelgeuse is so big that before the bullet travels completely around it and back to the starting point, the boy will be seventy years old.

Yet Betelgeuse is not the largest star of all. Astronomers say the largest stars have diameters of about 1 billion miles, 1,000 times larger than our sun.

Our star, besides being middle-sized, is also middle-aged. Like a man or woman thirty to thirty-five years old, it is about halfway through its life. But scientists know that stars don't live forever and earth won't always have

Star island—top view. Stars are not scattered evenly across the sky. They gather in groups of millions of stars called galaxies. Galaxies come in many shapes. This is an example of a spiral galaxy called M 101. Millions of stars, many like our sun, appear in this photograph. They are slowly turning around the hub, or center. This galaxy looks much like our Milky Way. If it were the Milky Way, our sun would be in one of the arms far from the hub. Dark lanes between the arms hold clouds of dust in which new stars may be forming.

U.S. NAVY

Star island—side view. The hub of this spiral galaxy (NGC 5194) probably holds many old red giants and black dwarf stars. The arms hold young blue stars and clouds of gas and dust from which new stars will be born. Gas and dust prevent astronomers on earth from looking into these clouds. But new telescopes will be able to look inside the clouds to discover what is happening there.

a star. The end of the sun story is already written. Our sun is burning itself out.

How stars die and how they are born are processes that astronomers are only beginning to understand. What they are learning with the help of new telescopes and other instruments is amazing, they say. Unbelievable. We are discovering marvels in the heavens that we never dreamed of.

20

Star cluster. Instead of spreading out, some stars come together in groups that look like balls, or clusters, from earth. This galaxy, called 47 Tucanae, is not visible in America or Europe. A telescope in Chile, South America, took the photograph. Star clusters like this hold between 10,000 and 1,000,000 stars. There is probably little gas or dust in the space between the stars.

Out in cold and dark space, scientists have discovered:

• Stars blinking on and off as they spin faster than a toy top—thirty times each *second*.

• Stars so heavy that a sugar-cube lump of their soil weighs *1 billion tons,* so heavy that the lump would sink right through earth and out the other side.

• Stars that blow up in explosions so great that their light shines brighter than all other stars around them, like one flashlight shining brighter than all the lights of a great city.

• Stars that disappear and become black holes in space. Black holes? One of the most mysterious happenings in the universe, scientists say. So far we're not really sure they exist. We think they do. But we haven't found one—yet. It's not easy finding a star that has eaten itself up and disappeared. Special telescopes on spacecraft orbiting the earth are looking for black holes. These strange objects will change many of our ideas about the universe.

The study of stars and how they live and die is helping scientists ask another important question: Is there life in outer space? Are there "people" or other living beings on planets turning around other stars? It's very possible, they say.

Finally, by understanding the life of stars, scientists have begun to understand sun power. This power makes life on earth possible. We can never know enough about the star that controls all life and energy on earth. This power makes the universe tick on and on like a fine watch.

Some people say they have a lucky star. But the truth is that everyone on earth has a lucky star. It's called the sun.

Two

A Birthday Cake Big as Twenty-one Football Fields

If we wanted to bake a birthday cake for our star, we would have to put 5 billion candles on it. *That* is how many years our star has given light and warmth to our planet—five followed by nine zeros: 5,000,000,000. To hold all those candles, the cake would have to be about as big as twenty-one football fields!

Five billion is another star number that is almost impossible to understand. We understand hundreds and thousands, maybe even millions if we talk about the cost of a new ship or airplane. But a *billion* of anything is not something that we come across every day.

However, in reading about how stars are born and die, we have to think in terms of billions because the life of most stars covers billions of years. So we'll try to imagine the 5-billion-year life of our star—from the time it "turned on" to today—like this:

Let's say that a snail sets out on a trip here on earth

that will take 5 billion years. It starts at New York and heads west. In the first year, it travels one inch. That's right—one *inch*. At this "speed," it would take about five and a half *years* to crawl across the page these words are printed on.

Year after year after year, the snail moves west—one inch by one inch by one inch. In the first million years it would crawl sixteen miles. Is there another town about sixteen miles from your home? That's how far it would go in 1 million years.

For the snail to crawl to Chicago would take about 50 million years. Ahead wait the Rocky Mountains, then the Pacific Ocean, China, Russia, and the countries of Europe. Across each of these places it travels at a steady one inch each year. By the time it passed through Italy and entered Spain it would have been crawling for about 5 *billion* years.

That is how long our star has been shining. Five billion years ago our star "turned on." No one has ever seen a star turn on, but astronomers who know where to point telescopes can practically see stars being born. These scientists look into great clouds of gas and dust floating in space. Dark spots or balls—where the dust and gas are thickest in the clouds—may be stars about to be born.

Astronomers say that a star doesn't light up all at once, like a lamp clicking on and lighting up a room. Instead, it happens slowly, something like a lantern turning on in a tent. The lantern begins to glow, then slowly gets brighter and brighter until the whole tent fills with light. When our star turned on, it began as a giant cloud of gas floating in dark space. The cloud was mostly hydrogen, a very light gas and the most common gas in the universe. For 10 million years, the hydrogen cloud contracted—drew together. What made the cloud

Stars about to "turn on." A gas cloud glows in a group of stars called Serpens. Dark spots inside the cloud may be stars that have formed but have not yet "turned on." Astronomers have found gases swirling and churning in these dark lanes.

contract? Gravity. From a wispy cloud billions of miles wide, gravity pulled the cloud in until it became a ball about the size of our star or sun today.

Gravity plays an important role in the story of how stars are born and, as we shall see later, how they die.

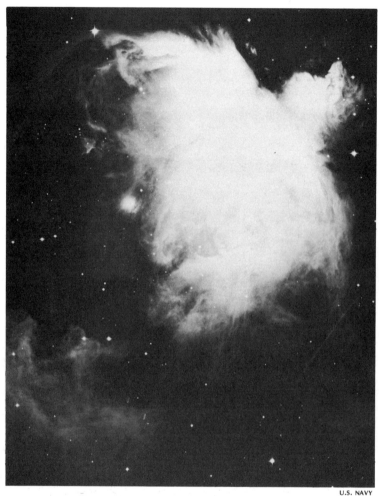

Birthplace of stars. The great nebula in the group of stars called Orion. We see this cloud as a star because it is so far away in space. But it is really a huge cloud of gas, mostly hydrogen. Astronomers say it is thick enough to form into a star or stars. When young stars begin to glow red, astronomers on earth know they have been born. The cloud is lighted from the inside by four very hot new stars. Our star, the sun, was born about five billion years ago in a cloud of dust and gas like Orion.

When we think of gravity, we usually think of that force here on earth—that *pull*—that draws us down when we jump off a step or over a bush. Without gravity, we could jump and never come down. We would drift up, up, up into the sky. Gravity pulls like a magnet. It holds us onto the earth.

Most people know the story of how Isaac Newton first came to think of gravity about three hundred years ago. One day he was sitting under an apple tree. An apple dropped on his head. "Aha!" he was supposed to have said. "That's gravity! The large earth attracted the small apple." At that point he rubbed his head and began writing the law of gravitation—about how objects are drawn together.

The story has become a folk tale, even though it didn't happen just that way. Newton was, however, a young man of twenty-two in 1664, when he began working out the law of gravitation. He became one of the greatest scientists the world has ever known. The law of gravitation he worked out is still used.

The first part of his law—high school students learn this in science class—says that the pull of gravity depends on the mass of an object. The more mass, the more pull. (Mass, remember, is the amount of material in an object.) Every particle of mass on earth—every rock and every grain of sand—has a tiny gravitational pull. Put all the sand, rock, and other material in the earth together, and the total mass adds up to the overall gravitational pull of earth. Newton's apple dropped toward earth—or the earth drew the apple toward it—because its mass was greater than the apple's. Thus, the earth had more pull.

But while Newton showed us how to measure gravity, he didn't tell us what gravity *is*.

Today, some 250 years after Newton died, we still

don't know what gravity is—or how to control it. We can control other kinds of energy—like electricity, radio waves, and nuclear power, for example. We can switch them on and off. But not gravity. We can't turn it on, switch it off, stop it, start it, slow it down, speed it up, store it in batteries, make it in a laboratory, or destroy it with bombs. Nor can we block it. It passes through thick lead as easily as it passes through the floors of our homes.

Gravity reaches everywhere on earth, and it also operates in space. It holds the moon in orbit around the earth. It controls the paths of Venus, Mars, earth, and the other planets around the sun. And it keeps our star and all other stars in place in the heavens. No two stars could ever crash together because gravity holds each one in place.

Not only does gravity control all objects in space, but it helps stars form. Over millions of years some of the atoms of hydrogen in the gas cloud floating in space bumped together, stuck, and formed a tiny mass. The gravity in this speck drew in other wandering atoms, and bits of dust floating in space. From a wispy cloud billions of miles wide, the cloud contracted to a dense, dark —and very hot—ball about 1 million miles in diameter.

Why was the ball of hydrogen hot? Space is cold, a couple of hundred degrees below zero. Why wasn't the hydrogen ball as cold as space around it?

Because the core of the ball was filled with furious activity—atoms of hydrogen bumping, rubbing, swirling, churning, and boiling as gravity slowly drew them closer and closer together in a smaller and smaller space. The friction—the rubbing together—of all those trillions of hydrogen atoms made the ball hotter and hotter. The heat rose to 10 million degrees Fahrenheit in its outer coat, 20 million degrees in its inner layer, and 27 million degrees in its center or core. When the temperature in the core reached that tremendous temperature, something happened.

If it had been possible to watch the gas ball for a few thousand years or so, we would have seen an amazing sight—the birth of a star. First, a dim glow deep inside, like the headlight of a car in thick fog. Next, the entire

Horse in the heavens. Astronomers call this dark shape the Horsehead Nebula. A huge cloud of dust and gas, it hides millions of stars shining behind it. These dark clouds are common in the universe.

ball beginning to glow—red, then orange. Finally, a steady glowing yellow, the color of our star today.

What happened inside the ball?

The heat and pressure at the core caused a change in the hydrogen atoms. The nuclei—or cores—of the atoms mashed together with such force that they changed into something entirely different. Two hydrogen atoms fused—joined together—and created one atom of helium.

Fusion is one of nature's grand gestures of creation, one of its most amazing magic acts. Like a magician snapping his fingers—abracadabra!—and changing a red scarf into a canary, nature changes one thing into something entirely different. Presto chango! Hydrogen into helium! For hundreds of years scientists wondered how the sun gave off heat and light. Only in the last fifty years or so have we known. Only now can we applaud and appreciate this astonishing act of creation in the theater of the heavens.

Every magic act has an explanation; here is what happens in the fusion process. The weight of the new helium atom is *less* than the combined weight of the two hydrogen atoms that fused. Think about this for a moment. It's the innermost secret of what makes the sun shine. If two balls of clay, each weighing one pound, are mashed together, the weight of the new ball should be two pounds, right? Right. But this doesn't happen with the two hydrogen atoms. In the intense heat of the sun's core, that extra bit of hydrogen that doesn't become helium is transformed into pure energy—heat and light. This energy floods from the core of the sun to the surface and spreads out from the gas ball through dark space for millions of miles.

This process is called a thermonuclear reaction. It is the same process that takes place when a hydrogen

Bubble of gas. Astronomers say jets of super-hot gas start deep inside the sun and work up to the surface. Then they flare thousands of miles into space. One flare like the one in this picture equals the power of a million exploding hydrogen bombs. At right, a giant bubble blows out from the sun and begins to expand in space.

bomb explodes. In the sun, of course, more than a few specks of hydrogen are involved. Every second the sun's furnace changes 657 million tons of hydrogen into 652½ million tons of helium. The remaining 4½ tons are the hydrogen that changes to heat and light.

31

Scientists once thought that the sun's energy came from something that was burning, like a fire in a fireplace. Today, however, we know that the sun's light and heat come from thermonuclear reactions in the core of the sun, the miracle of transforming matter (hydrogen) into energy.

Hydrogen bomb. The most powerful man-made explosion on earth is a hydrogen bomb. This photograph shows a fireball from a hydrogen bomb explosion from 50 miles away. The fireball is two miles high. This is the kind of explosion that takes place at the center of the sun. The energy from the explosion moves up to the surface of the sun, then out into space as sunlight. On earth, 93 million miles away, we feel the energy of these explosions as heat and see them as light. If this energy did not come to earth, no life could exist here.

U.S. AIR FORCE

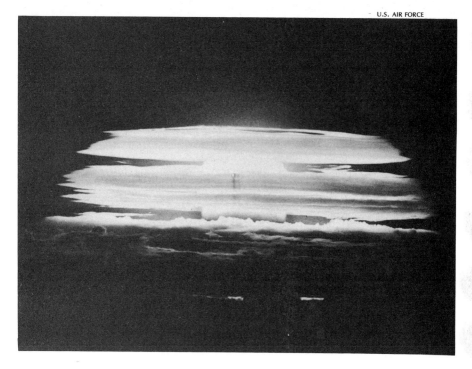

Although millions of tons of hydrogen are involved in this process each second, the earth receives only a few pounds—about four—of the energy given off. The rest radiates (spreads) out from the sun into space in all directions. But those four pounds of energy per second make life on earth possible.

Besides turning the sun "on," the thermonuclear reaction did something else. It stopped gravity from pulling the hydrogen ball in. The power of the reactions in the core pushed out, out, out—tried to make the ball expand. Gravity resisted, pulled the ball in, in, in. At some moment the two forces exactly balanced each other—the outward flow of energy balancing the inward pull of gravity.

When this balance happened, our star settled down. It became stable and dependable. With its steady warm light day after day, millions of years after millions of years, life could begin on earth 93 million miles away in space.

From earth, the sun seems to be glowing quietly. But telescopes give us a close-up look and show us something different: great whirling winds of fire whipping and churning its surface into a choppy sea of flame; giant burning bubbles blasting into space; streamers of fire leaping tens of thousands of miles, then bending in graceful curves and splashing back onto the surface.

On January 21, 1974, astronaut Ed Gibson was orbiting earth in Skylab 3. He was looking at the sun through a special telescope. On the surface he saw a spot of white light. Seconds later a finger of burning gas raced up from the spot in a great curve and disappeared into space.

Back on earth, Gibson told other scientists about the gas jet. "We saw the birth and total life of a sun flare! We have observed a flare as never before!"

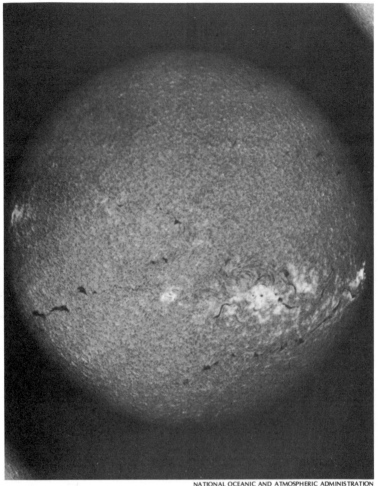

Sea of flames. From earth, the sun looks like a smooth orange or yellow ball. But close up the sun's surface looks like what it really is, a stormy sea of burning gas. This photograph was taken by a telescope in a spacecraft, Skylab 3, on July 5, 1974. It shows "rice grains," light and dark spots like grains of rice. The light "grains" and spots may be columns of hot gas moving to the surface. The dark "grains" and spots are probably columns of gas sinking from the surface down to the core of the sun.

Spots on the sun. These sunspots may be slightly cooler gas coming to the sun's surface. They last for a few days to several months. The large group of spots at right are about 40,000 miles across—about five times the size of earth. Sunspots are slightly cooler than the surface around them—6,000° F. compared with 10,000° F. Most sunspots are about the size of earth. The largest, however, could swallow Jupiter, a planet ten times earth's size. The number of sunspots seems to change every eleven years, but scientists don't know why.

NATIONAL OCEANIC AND ATMOSPHERIC ADMINISTRATION

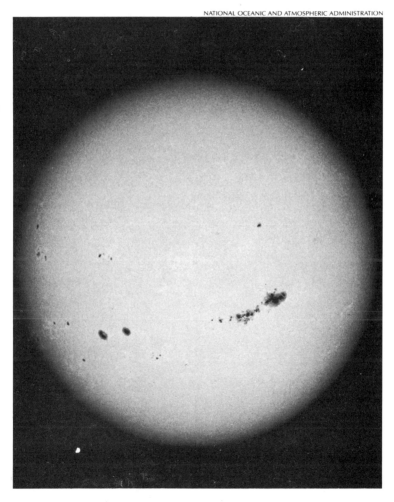

Mighty gas flare. A telescope on Skylab 4 photographed a powerful gas flare on the sun on December 19, 1973. The jet of gas leaped 367,000 miles across the sun before splashing back onto its surface. The flare looks like a twist of gas trying to unwind itself.

Tongue of fire. Skylab astronauts photographed this flaming tongue of gas on August 21, 1974. The flare reached a height of 350,000 miles. Astronomers say the power in this one flare would be enough for all people on earth from the time of Christ to the present—and maybe for the next 2,000 years as well.

Scientists say the energy of one of these mighty flares equals a million hydrogen bombs going off all at once.

Our star is a giant ball of superhot glowing gas—and it is anything but quiet. Astronomers today can listen to the sun with special radio receivers. It spits and sputters and crackles and roars, they say. The gas in the ball is loose and flowing around itself. At the equator the sun turns once in twenty-five days; at the poles it turns once in thirty-four days. Its hydrogen fuel will keep it warming earth for another 5 billion years. But someday all the hydrogen will be gone, burned up. Stars don't live forever. What will happen then?

But hold on, you may very well ask: How can astronomers be so smart? How do they know so much about stars? How can they tell what our star is made of? About one hundred years ago scientists said it was a ball of glowing coal. Before that they said it was glowing iron. Today they *say* it's a ball of hydrogen. But how do they *know?* Our star is millions of miles away in space, and astronomers are right here on earth. Who knows? Maybe the sun *is* a ball of burning coal!

Good questions—and astronomers were a long time in finding the answers. The answers had to wait for a remarkable instrument, the spectroscope, to be invented.

The spectroscope is a very simple instrument. Have you ever seen a rainbow in the sky after a rain? Then you already know something about spectroscopes and how they help astronomers learn about stars far out in space.

Three

The Code of Starlight— and How Astronomers Decoded It

It was a sunny day in the year 1666. Isaac Newton, the English scientist who first worked out the law of gravitation, began an experiment in his laboratory.

First, he closed the shutters in front of the window. The room became dark. Then he drilled a small hole in one shutter. When he removed the drill, a beam of bright sunlight came through the hole. In front of the beam, he held a triangle of glass—a prism. This is what he wrote in his notebook: "It was . . . very pleasing . . . to view the vivid and intense colours. . . ."

Across the room, the "colours" fanned out on the wall—a rainbow.

Most of us have seen a rainbow. After a rain shower the clouds part and the sun shines. The sunlight passes through drops of water in the air. The drops act like tiny prisms. Instead of passing directly through the drops the way it passes through glass, the light is refracted

—bent—by the shape of the drops. Bent light separates into its parts, into all the colors that make it up. A rainbow appears.

Newton's experiment proved something very important. Light is not white. Instead, it is a blend of seven different colors: red, orange, yellow, green, blue, dark blue, and violet. He called the rainbow a spectrum —from the Latin word meaning specter, a phantom or ghost.

But what did the spectrum mean? Newton didn't know. He *thought* light was made up of particles— he called them corpuscles. Different corpuscles made up the different colors. But he couldn't prove his idea.

A hundred and fifty years passed. Then another scientist took Newton's findings to the next step.

Joseph von Fraunhofer was a German optician—a maker of eyeglasses. In 1814 he repeated Newton's experiment, but he made one change. Between the hole in the shutter and the prism he held a piece of metal. The metal was cut with a narrow slit. Now each color in the rainbow on the far wall was cut by black lines. Fraunhofer made careful drawings of the lines. But what did the lines in each color mean? The lines were like a code. But neither Fraunhofer nor anyone else knew how to decode them.

A half century went by. In 1859 another German scientist, Gustav Kirchhoff, discovered the secret of the mysterious lines.

Working with Robert Bunsen, Kirchhoff performed an experiment. This experiment started astronomers on the way to answering many questions about the stars, to decoding the message of starlight.

In their laboratory, the two scientists took a chunk of iron and heated it white hot—incandescent. When the light from the glowing metal passed through a slit and then through a prism, it produced a pattern of color and lines.

The two scientists then heated other materials—like calcium and phosphorus—and gases like hydrogen and oxygen in corked bottles. Each material, they found, gave off its own pattern of lines. Each one had its own special "fingerprint." No two patterns of spectral lines were alike. Thus, the code of starlight was decoded, and one of the most important scientific instruments of all time was finally born: the spectroscope.

The code of starlight. A white beam of starlight is made up of many colors. By breaking up the beam into its colors, astronomers can tell what a star is made of—hydrogen, helium, oxygen, nitrogen, iron, calcium, and many other materials. Each material makes its own "fingerprint" in the band of colors, the spectrum. Astronomers read these spectrums and learn much about stars millions of miles away in space.

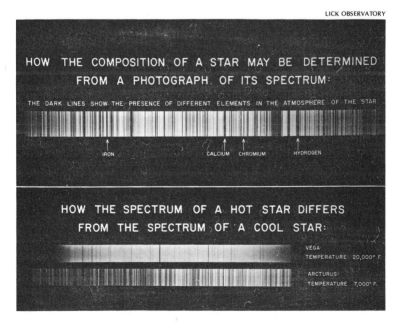

HOW THE COMPOSITION OF A STAR MAY BE DETERMINED FROM A PHOTOGRAPH OF ITS SPECTRUM:

THE DARK LINES SHOW THE PRESENCE OF DIFFERENT ELEMENTS IN THE ATMOSPHERE OF THE STAR

IRON   CALCIUM CHROMIUM   HYDROGEN

HOW THE SPECTRUM OF A HOT STAR DIFFERS FROM THE SPECTRUM OF A COOL STAR:

VEGA
TEMPERATURE 20,000° F.

ARCTURUS
TEMPERATURE 7,000° F.

Astronomers began fitting spectroscopes to telescopes. The light of a star, after entering the telescope, passed through a narrow slit and then was recorded on film. By examining the lines on the film, scientists could tell what materials a star far out in space was made of. It was almost as easy as examining a piece of that star under a microscope. Materials in stars—like hydrogen, carbon, silicon, iron—could be found right here on earth, so scientists recognized their special "fingerprints."

Today astronomers have become even more skilled at reading the messages carried by a beam of starlight. Besides telling them what materials are in a star, the spectroscope helps them calculate:

- A star's temperature.
- The strength of its gravity.
- Its weight.
- The speed at which it is moving away from or toward earth.
- How fast it turns.
- Whether it has a magnetic field.

With the spectroscope, astronomers learned to identify different kinds of stars: hot stars; cool stars; giant stars that are using up their hydrogen fuel fast and whose life spans are running out; small stars that are using their hydrogen slowly and whose life span will cover billions of years.

Our star, as we know, has another 5 billion years of life left. What will happen when it uses up the last wisp of its hydrogen?

It won't go out—puff!—like a candle snuffing out. Instead, it will cool slowly, over many millions of years. Finally, it will burn itself out and become a dead cinder in space, a burned-out star.

Here's how it will happen: The sun's core will use up its hydrogen first and become helium ash, but the hydrogen in the outer layers will continue to "burn." Our star's color will change from yellow to red as its temperature cools slightly.

But the heat in these outer layers will make our star expand. It will grow like a giant red balloon puffing up larger and larger. Over a billion years it will grow 250 times larger than it is now, like a pea blowing up to the size of a bicycle wheel.

As it grows into a red giant like Betelgeuse, its powerful gravity will draw the two closest planets, Mercury and Venus, onto its surface. Much like pebbles dropping into a pond, these planets will disappear into the sun's fiery depths. On earth, whole forests would have burst into flame. Then the hot breath of our star will make lead flow like molasses. Steel girders of bridges will bend like soft putty. Eventually the oceans will begin to boil away.

And people? What will happen to people living on earth? By that time people will most surely have left earth. They will have long since boarded spaceships and fled to planets far away from the scorching heat.

For 100 million years, our dying star will use up its hydrogen. As fuel becomes low, as the outward thrust of heat lessens, gravity will gradually take over—tugging, pulling, drawing the remaining gas to the core.

Over thousands of centuries, as the helium atoms in the core fuse into carbon, the steady pull of gravity will pack the core into a giant ball of superhot ash. In time the enormous red giant will shrink to a ball the size of earth. As the star shrinks, its temperature will go up, and its color will change—from red to yellow to white. Scientists call these dying stars white dwarfs.

For a few million more years our shrunken star will

glow with heat. As it slowly cools, it will change color again—from white to yellow to orange to red. One day the last of its fires will burn low and flicker out. Then it will become dark, a cinder drifting in black and cold space. A black dwarf.

As our star cools, so will earth. Everlasting cold and darkness will settle on our planet. Our earth with its dark moon will continue to orbit a dead star. Nothing—people, animals, plants—will ever live here again.

Scientists say that 10 out of every 100 stars in the universe are either white or black dwarfs—dead stars that have spent the last of their fuel. Gravity has packed them so tight that a golf ball filled with their soil would weigh as much as an ocean liner.

Four

Stars That Blow Up

In China, about 500 years before Columbus discovered America, on the morning of July 4, 1054, Yang Wei-te was standing in his garden, looking at the sky. It was still dark; the sun had not come up. Yang Wei-te was an astronomer. He knew—and could name—every star in the sky.

This morning he saw a new star. It was in the east over Khaifeng. Yang had never seen it before. It was as yellow and bright as the planet Venus.

After the sun came up, Yang could still see the strange star. How is it possible? he asked. How can a star shine during the day?

Yang Wei-te was not the only astronomer who saw the new star. Another Chinese astronomer also saw it. He wrote: "It shone so brightly that objects could be seen by its light." Still another astronomer wrote these words into his record: "Its light illuminated the horizon and . . . its brightness was a little more than a quarter of the brightness of the moon."

For the next twenty-three days the star was visible during the day, even in summer sunshine. At night it was

Exploding star. An astronomer in Atlanta, Georgia, took these photographs of an exploding star, Nova Cygni, in August 1975. Thousands of people saw Nova Cygni without telescopes. It was about as bright as the brightest stars in the

brighter than any other star. Only after 650 nights did it finally fade. Yang Wei-te called it a guest star. Like a visiting guest, it had stayed for a while and then left.

Astronomers today know what Yang Wei-te and the other astronomers saw in the sky nearly 1,000 years ago—an exploding star. An exploding star is an amazing sight. But what is even more amazing is that our astronomers today *still see the same explosion.* They call it the Crab Nebula (neb-you-lah). A nebula is a cloud of dust and gas.

Far out in space, the Crab Nebula is a beautiful glowing cloud of blue-white gas streaked with red lines. It is still expanding at the speed of 700 miles each

Big Dipper. Nova Cygni faded rapidly. The first photograph was made on August 31. The second on September 2. The third on September 9. The last photograph was made on October 11.

second—and this 900 years after the star exploded! Each day it expands 60 million miles. Today it is bigger than our star's entire family of nine planets.

Astronomers see an exploding star in our galaxy every ten years or so. But they believe there may be many more, maybe twenty-five to forty each year. Many go unseen because they are too far from earth—or dust clouds in space hide them from our telescopes.

Some stars become thousands of times brighter when they explode. These exploding stars are called novas. Novas fade in a few weeks. Astronomers have seen novas in 1901, 1918, 1925, 1934, 1942, and 1975.

Some stars, however, become a million times brighter

when they explode. They take years, even thousands of years to fade—like the Crab Nebula. Because of their brightness, astronomers call these stars supernovas.

Supernovas are the most spectacular sight in the sky. For several months, they may shine as bright as 200 million suns, as bright as an entire galaxy of stars! They can even be seen without a telescope. But they are rare; they don't happen very often. In the last 1,000 years, astronomers have counted only four—in 1006, 1054, 1572, and 1604.

Why do stars explode? If you asked an astronomer, he or she might answer: Good question! We would like to know, too. We can see what happens when a star explodes, but we don't know for sure *why* it explodes. What may happen is something like this:

Stars that explode seem to be giant stars much larger than our star. These giants begin to die when the hydrogen in their cores has changed to helium and the core begins to cool slightly.

In time the heat flowing out from the slowly cooling core begins to decrease. It can no longer puff up the heavy outer layers of gas hundreds of thousands or millions of miles thick. All the while gravity has been gently tugging at the layers of gas. At some moment the steady pull becomes stronger than the outward push of heat. The gas layers grow thicker and heavier. Gradually they begin to fall inward, collapsing toward the core.

Pulled in by gravity that now has nothing to stop it, the outer layers of gas rush faster and faster toward the core, crushing and mashing it. Imagine our earth crushing together into a ball only 600 feet wide—about two football fields—in two or three seconds. This is the terrible squeezing, the enormous packing together, that happens to the cores of these huge stars.

As the outer layers collapse, the weight of the gas

—the inrushing of billions of trillions of tons—causes the star to heat up. In one instant its temperature shoots up millions of degrees. Unable to tolerate this enormous temperature, the outer layers blast off in a stupendous explosion, kicking out flame and light and gas and dust. The sky around flares white hot with the power of a million suns. The star that took millions of years to form from a cloud of gas and dust, that gave off light and heat for tens of millions of years, has destroyed itself in a brief instant.

What is left of the star? The core, maybe ten miles across.

Astronomers have given a name to these small cores. They call them neutron (new-tron) stars. They say that neutron stars are among the most surprising discoveries ever to happen in astronomy. A teaspoonful of a neutron star's dust, packed under the terrible squeeze of collapsing layers of gas, weighs 1 *billion* tons, as much as 200 million elephants, an elephant for every man, woman, and child in the United States.

What would happen if we could take a pebble from a neutron star and drop it on earth? That pebble would be so heavy that it would fall right into the ground and not stop. It would fall all the way through earth and out the other side.

The gravity of a neutron star is so strong—100 billion times stronger than earth's gravity—that everything on its surface is pulled as smooth as a rubber ball. A mountain on a neutron star, if one were there, would be no more than an inch high. But to climb it would take an entire lifetime!

Two astronomers in England discovered neutron stars. In July 1967 a young college graduate from Northern Ireland, Jocelyn Bell, was working at an observatory in Cambridge, England. She was using a radio telescope, a

A star that turns on and off. This neutron star is in the heart of the Crab Nebula, trillions of miles away in space. It flashes on and off thirty times a second. In the top picture, it is on. In the bottom picture, it is off.

special telescope that listens to radio waves from stars. (See Chapter 6.)

One day she was looking at radio waves being traced on a 400-foot-long strip of paper. Suddenly she noticed something strange. The pen was recording regular signals every one and a third seconds.

Impossible, Miss Bell thought. Radio signals from outer space were never regular. They came in as static—cracklings, hissings, rumblings—never as steady signals.

She asked her professor to look at the paper. Professor Antony Hewish was just as amazed. Sure enough, the signals were coming in every one and a third seconds. They looked at each other. Was it possible that "people" on another planet were sending signals to earth?

Over many weeks Miss Bell and Professor Hewish timed the signals. They were as steady as a clock. And they were coming from deep in space! What could they be?

Miss Bell and Professor Hewish asked other astronomers at Cambridge to look at the place in the sky where the signals were coming from. The place was the Crab Nebula. The object giving off the signals? The *core* of the star that had exploded 900 years earlier. It was flashing on and off thirty times each second and sending radio signals every one and a third seconds!

The astronomers could hardly believe what they were seeing. In fact, they kept the discovery from the public for many weeks until they could study it more thoroughly. Here was a tiny star, only a dozen or so miles across, shining brighter than our sun. It was like a searchlight going around and around, sending out flashes of light, spinning faster than a toy top. To stand the terrific force of spinning 1,800 times each minute and not flying apart, the astronomers figured that the crust had to be a trillion times stronger than steel!

Why does a neutron star spin so fast?

Large stars turn slowly—say, once every thirty days. After a star blows off its outer layers, the tiny core absorbs all the spin that kept the larger star turning. Have you ever watched a skater spin on ice? With arms stretched out, the skater spins slowly. But when the skater pulls in his or her arms, the spin speeds up.

This is what happened to the core of the star in the Crab Nebula. When its outer layers blew off, it pulled in on itself and began to spin faster and faster until it was turning thirty times each second.

Scientists all over the world were surprised at Miss Bell and Professor Hewish's discovery. No one really believed that anything as strange as a neutron star existed, though their existence had been predicted mathematically. Today astronomers can point to about 150 neutron stars.

Will astronauts ever land on a tiny neutron star and explore it, try to climb its inch-high mountains? Not likely. Said one astronomer:

If an astronaut, more foolish than brave, came as close to a neutron star as we are to the moon, he would meet a horrible death. The star's gravity would pull him to shreds. To explore a neutron star, to escape its powerful gravity, his spaceship would have to travel past it so fast that he would have only a thousandth of a second to glimpse it. Then he *might* survive!

Five

The Riddle of Utmost Gravity

Stars that wink on and off! Stars whose soil weighs a billion tons! Stars with mountains one inch high! These are marvels hard for us "earthlings" to understand. "The universe is not only queerer than we suppose, but queerer than we can suppose!" said a British scientist, J. B. S. Haldane.

But hold on, there's more! As scientists try to understand what happens when stars die, they have come up with something that is strange beyond belief: black holes—bottomless pits in space.

No black hole has ever been found. Yet many scientists believe they exist. So far proof that they exist lies mostly in mathematics, but solid proof may soon be coming.

The key to understanding black holes begins with Newton's law of gravitation. Students in high school, after learning the first part of Newton's law—all things in the universe attract all other things, and the strength of an object's gravity depends on its mass—learn the second part: The strength of gravity is inversely proportional to the square of the distance between two objects.

What does this mean? Simply that the farther apart two objects are, the weaker will be their attraction for each other.

The important word in Newton's law, though, is "square." Here's why:

If two objects move apart, their attraction for each other becomes less. Double the distance, and their attraction decreases by four—two times two. Triple the distance, and it goes down by nine—three times three.

"Square" in mathematics means a number times itself. There is always some attraction between two objects in space, but the strength of that attraction goes down by the *square* of the distance between them.

So far, so good. But what happens when two objects come closer together? The law has to work then, too, and it does. As objects come closer together, their gravity increases—grows ever stronger—by the square of their distance. And this is at the root of how scientists account for these strange objects—black holes—in space.

When a giant star uses up its fuel, the outward push from thermonuclear reactions in its core lessens. Its balance is destroyed, and the inpull of gravity takes over. The star begins to shrink as the outer layers fall toward the center. As the atoms pack together, the space between them lessens. Their attraction to each other grows. It multiplies by the square of the space between them. The more jamming together, the more gravity is created. At some point gravity begins to run wild.

The mass of a star determines how far it will shrink. Our sun will shrink to a white dwarf about the size of earth. Its mass can develop only so much gravity, no more. The collapse stops itself because parts of the atom repel each other and resist the pressures of gravity.

A star larger than our sun, with more mass, may shrink to a dense neutron star a dozen miles wide before the collapse stops.

But giant stars—stars with twenty or thirty times the mass of our sun—will continue to shrink. They develop such gravitational force that even the forces within the atoms and their nuclei cannot resist it. Once started, the shrinking can't stop. Gravity swallows up the star. Its final moments may take less than a second. The star disappears—"winks" out. Its light vanishes. It becomes a black hole. Nothing is left of the star, but powerful gravity.

What's inside a black hole?

Impossible to tell, say astronomers. It may take thousands of years, if ever, before we can move into a black hole to find out what's happening there. But let's say we're going to try. What would happen if, with what we know today, we tried to enter a black hole?

Our spaceship stops in space. An astronaut, carrying a flashlight, leaves the spaceship. From a distance he sees clouds of bright gas circling the deepest blackness he has ever seen, like water racing around a whirlpool into a black pit.

As he gets within several thousand miles of the black hole, he feels the first gentle tug of gravity. Later, within several miles of the black hole, its gravity, like the arm of an octopus, grasps him. Now there is no going back.

He begins moving toward the hole, slowly at first and then faster. Far behind him, the lights of his spaceship drift farther and farther away. So strong does the gravity become, so eager is it to claim him, that his body begins to stretch out, like a piece of soft taffy. If he is six feet

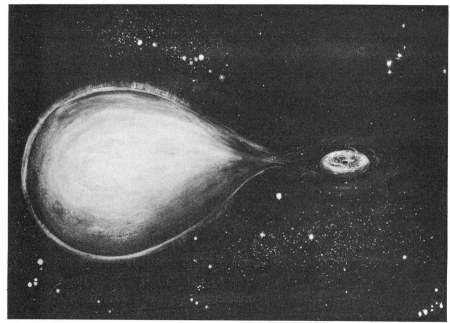

Black hole. A painting of what a black hole, called Cygnus X-1, may look like. The black hole is at the center of the "doughnut" at right. It is invisible, but astronomers believe it is there because of the hot gases swirling around it. The powerful gravity of the black hole draws gas from the large star at left. In time the large star will be pulled apart and disappear into the black hole. Anything entering a black hole disappears from sight.

tall, his body stretches to seven feet, then to eight feet. Then it begins to stretch even thinner, long as a string of spaghetti. His heart and stomach—all his organs —stretch like rubber balloons.

Frantically he signals to his friends on the spaceship. Once every second he flashes a distress call: dot-dot-dot, dash-dash-dash, dot-dot-dot. S O S in radio code. A call for help.

On the spaceship, his friends see the flashes. They know he is in trouble. But there is nothing they can do. Helplessly they watch the flashes. They draw farther and farther away.

Now something strange happens. The spaceman continues to press the button of his flashlight once every second. But the flashes of light take longer and longer to reach the spaceship. First, a minute between flashes. Then a quarter hour. An hour. Finally, as the spaceman continues to speed into the black hole, still blinking his flashlight once each second, a whole year passes before the flash of light escapes the black hole's gravity. Then 1,000 years. Finally, no light at all escapes. The beam from the astronaut's flashlight circles around the edge of the black hole and then is sucked into its depths. Nothing can escape the powerful pull of the black hole's gravity, not even light.

Where does the black hole go? What is at the bottom of its lightless depths?

Astronomers can make only wild guesses. Some say these holes are pipelines or wormholes to other parts of the universe. If there are "people" on other planets in space, they may use black holes to zip from one place in the universe to another. Just as we have road maps to show us how to drive between states, these "people" may have maps showing how black holes go from one part of the universe to another. They may fly their spaceships into one end of a black hole and moments later get blown out the other end billions of miles away.

If black holes can't be seen through telescopes, then how do astronomers know they are out there? One way is to look for stars moving in a wobbly orbit instead of a smooth orbit. These stars may have black holes nearby. The gravity of the black hole tugs at the larger star and makes it wobble in its path.

Astronomers also have another way to find black holes. Sometimes a black hole draws off burning gas from a larger star. This gas moves faster and faster as it races around the black hole's edge. Soon it heats up to millions of degrees. Then it pours down the mouth of the black hole, like water pouring into the drain of a sink.

The heat from the speeding gas gives off a flood of energy waves called X rays which scatter through space. Fortunately X rays don't reach earth's surface. If they did, every person and probably every thing would burn to a crisp. Our air blanket stops these deadly rays from reaching us.

To measure X rays and find out where they are coming from, scientists send X-ray detectors on rockets and satellites above our air blanket. One such X-ray satellite was launched in 1970 from East Africa. Called *Uhuru*—an African word meaning freedom—it swept the sky with its tiny X-ray detectors. *Uhuru* found 339 X-ray sources—from exploding stars, from neutron stars, and possibly from black holes.

One powerful flow of X rays came from the constellation Cygnus—a group of stars called the Northern Cross. Astronomers named the source Cygnus X-1. It was near a bright supergiant twenty times our sun's mass.

Astronomers tested the light of the star with a spectroscope. They found that it was one of two stars moving around each other once every five and a half days and held together by their mutual gravitational attraction. But the second star was invisible. Scientists knew it was there, however, because of the intense X rays it gave off. The powerful gravity of the "dark companion" drew the gas from the supergiant across 13 million miles of space.

What's more, the supergiant wobbled in its orbit, perhaps because of the gravitational pull of its unseen neighbor.

Is Cygnus X-1 a black hole? Some scientists say yes, no doubt.

A final answer to the question may come soon. New telescopes on satellites orbiting the earth are pointing directly at Cygnus X-1. They are gathering information which may help scientists find the answer—the answer to the riddle of utmost gravity.

Some scientists believe there may be 1 black hole for every 100 stars. They say these black holes are slowly growing larger and larger as they feed on gas and dust drifting in space and from nearby stars.

Nothing can stop them from growing. In time everything in the universe will tumble into a black hole. Then the black holes will eat up each other, the larger holes feeding on the smaller holes.

If this happens, it will take trillions of years for everything in the universe to disappear. But by that time we will have learned all the dark secrets of black holes and how the human race can live with them—or perhaps *in* them.

Six

Windows into Space

What if you had to use only your eyes to learn about the world? Imagine how much you would miss. You couldn't use your fingers—your sense of touch—to feel the softness of a rabbit's fur or the heat of a pan on the stove. You wouldn't know if an apple was sweet or sour. Why? Because you couldn't taste it.

And think of all the things you wouldn't know about because you couldn't hear—bands playing and people telling stories. Nor would you know that a rose gave off perfume that you could smell and enjoy.

By using only your eyes, you could learn a lot about your world. But how much you would miss! With your other senses—taste, sound, touch, smell—you could learn so much more about the world.

For more than 300 years, astronomers used only one sense, their eyes, to learn about the heavens around earth. An Italian astronomer named Galileo put together an early telescope about the year 1610. Ever since astronomers used their eyes—and only their eyes—to learn about the universe. Astronomers didn't know they had other senses.

But fifty years ago a telephone company engineer made a strange discovery. He showed astronomers how to use their other senses to study the stars. Here is what happened:

Karl Jansky was a twenty-five-year-old engineer who worked for the Bell Telephone Laboratories in New Jersey. One day his boss came to him. Our radio messages from Europe are getting mixed up, the man said. There's too much static. We can't hear a thing! Find out what's causing this noise and what we can do about it.

The first thing to do, Jansky decided, was to find out what was causing the static. So he built a large antenna, the same kind of aerial a radio uses to receive radio programs. Jansky's antenna was a wood frame 100 feet long. He strung it with copper wires. Then he put wheels on the frame. The wheels turned the antenna on a track once every twenty minutes. By turning the antenna, Jansky could point it to any part of the sky.

By August 1931 Jansky knew what made the static. His antenna had picked up the crackling sounds of lightning. The lightning came from thunderstorms over the Atlantic Ocean. This noise mixed with radio messages coming from Europe. It made them hard to hear.

But below the static Jansky heard something else. He heard a soft hissing—*ssss*—like steam hissing from a kettle on a stove. Soon the young engineer learned what the strange hissing was: radio waves coming to earth from stars billions of miles out in space.

Jansky's copper-and-wood antenna opened a new field, radio astronomy. Before Jansky's discovery, everything astronomers knew about the stars came on beams of light which they "decoded." Now they had radio waves. They had a way to *listen* to the stars.

Today huge dish-shaped antennas—some as wide as a football field—listen to the stars. They hear the sounds

World's first radio telescope. Karl Jansky with the radio telescope he built in a field in New Jersey. The wooden frame supported a copper-wire antenna. Wheels from an old Ford car allowed the antenna to turn in a circle.

that stars make—sighs, sputterings, cracklings, rumblings, roarings. The signals are recorded on paper, then sorted by computer. In this way, astronomers have found new messages to decode. These messages hold new information about the stars.

With the radio telescope, astronomers had two "windows" to observe the universe—a light window and a radio window. Light waves and most radio waves could pass through the thick blanket of air around earth to deliver messages.

But then scientists asked an important question: What about other waves that stars send out—X rays, ultraviolet waves, infrared waves, and gamma waves?

Listening to the stars. In the 1930s, Karl Jansky discovered hissing sounds coming from the center of the Milky Way. In time he learned that these sounds were really radio waves sent out by stars. His findings allowed astronomers to expand their study of the stars. From seeing stars through optical telescopes only, they began to listen to radio signals that stars gave off. This began the new science of radio astronomy. Here Jansky points to the position on a chart of the heavens from which he first heard radio waves. This photo was taken in 1933.

These waves carry information, too. They travel billions of miles through space. Then, barely 100 miles up, the earth's air blanket stops them. They don't finish their journey.

Think of all we are missing, astronomers said, just because we can't receive these messages. It's like having a TV set with only two channels. If we could tune in on the other channels, how much more we would learn!

Then scientists hit on a way to record these messages from space. They sent up rockets and balloons high above the air blanket around earth. The rockets and balloons carried instruments that recorded these other "channels."

These instruments, like the radio telescope, opened even more "windows" into the universe. But there was one thing wrong. Balloons and rockets could keep the instruments up for only a short time—seconds or a few minutes. Astronomers needed a way to keep the instruments above the air blanket for days.

Then another major development took place: satellite astronomy. Scientists placed telescopes and other instruments on satellites and sent them into orbit around the earth. They recorded other energy waves coming from the stars. Radios on the satellites sent these signals to astronomers on earth.

Some discoveries these new instruments made were indeed surprising. In September 1975 a satellite found a star that suddenly began pouring out X rays. It had always been a quiet star. But now it was sending out five times more X rays than any other star. If X rays were visible like light waves, the star would shine like the moon.

What did this mean? Astronomers didn't know. But fortunately for us, one astronomer said, the star is trillions of miles away from earth. If it had been as close to

Modern radio telescope. The dish-shaped antenna of this radio telescope is 140 feet wide, about half a football field long. It can hear radio signals from stars trillions of miles away in space. Optical telescopes operate only at night, when the stars shine and the weather is clear. But radio telescopes operate in rain, in cloudy weather, and during the day. This radio telescope is in Green Bank, West Virginia.

earth as the nearest star, Alpha Centauri, only 26 trillion miles away, the X rays would have passed through our air blanket and quickly burned up our planet.

Soon new X-ray telescopes will be sent into orbit around earth. Called High-Energy Astronomy Observatories (HEAO), these telescopes, weighing three tons each, will search the sky for X rays. They will measure and map these energy waves given off by supernovas, neutron stars, and black holes.

X-ray sky. In December 1970, the *Uhuru* satellite went into orbit. High above earth's blanket of air, it located stars giving off X rays. Some of these stars—like CYG X-1 (Cygnus X-1)— may show the location of black holes. This is a map of the X-ray sky that astronomers drew from more than 160 X-ray stars that *Uhuru* found.

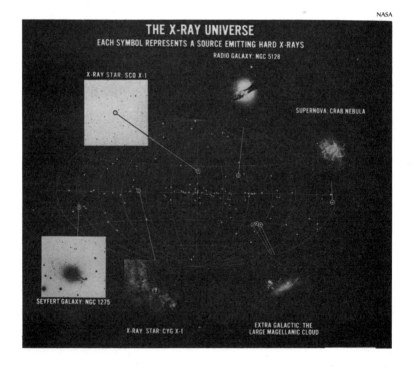

NASA

THE X-RAY UNIVERSE
EACH SYMBOL REPRESENTS A SOURCE EMITTING HARD X-RAYS
RADIO GALAXY: NGC 5128

X-RAY STAR: SCO X-1

SUPERNOVA: CRAB NEBULA

SEYFERT GALAXY: NGC 1275

X-RAY STAR: CYG X-1

EXTRA GALACTIC: THE
LARGE MAGELLANIC CLOUD

X-ray telescopes. By 1979, three new X-ray telescopes were to be sent into orbit 225 miles above earth to find, measure, and study exploding stars, clouds of gas and dust, neutron stars, and black holes. As long and as heavy as small trucks—18 to 20 feet long, 8 feet wide, 3 tons—the HEAOs (High-Energy Astronomy Observatories) orbit six months to a year. Solar cells will convert sunlight to electricity to run instruments.

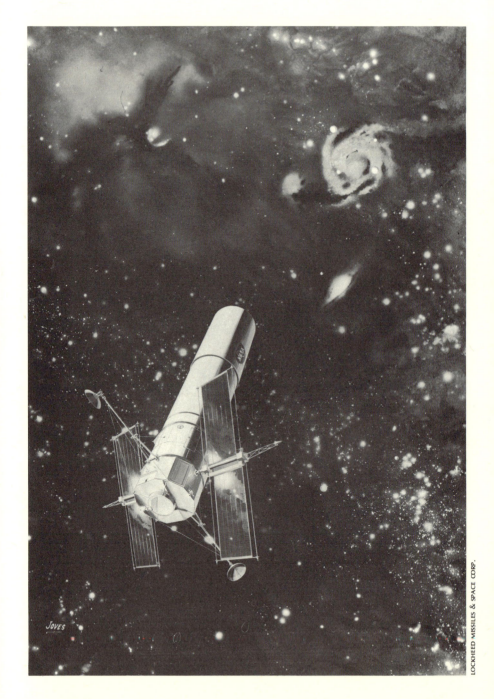

JOVES

68

Large space telescope.   In the early 1980s, astronomers expect to place this new telescope 310 miles above earth. In airless outer space, the telescope will look deep into the universe. It will see planets and galaxies seven times farther away than the finest telescopes on earth can see. It will weigh about 7½ tons, be 40 to 45 feet long, and 10 to 15 feet wide. Solar panels on the sides will make electricity to power its instruments. The LST will send pictures to earth by radio and TV. The LST will point at one star for thirty to forty hours at a time—like a rifle in Boston holding aim on a ten-cent piece in Washington, D.C.

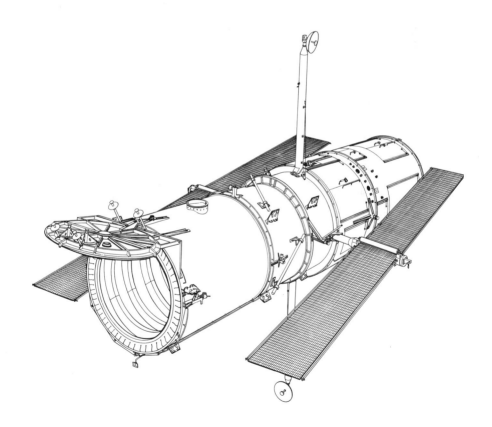

69

In the early 1980s another new telescope will go into orbit. The space shuttle will carry the space telescope 310 miles above earth. There, in air-free space, the forty-three-foot-long telescope will look seven times farther into space than the biggest telescope on earth. If it were placed in Washington, D.C., it could see the headlights of a car in Moscow, Russia. TV cameras will send pictures of what it sees to astronomers on earth. The big fourteen-foot-wide telescope will study how stars are born and how they die. It will give astronomers more information on how big the universe is, how old it is, how it began, and how it will probably end. It may discover objects deep in space that astronomers don't even know about. It may even be able to see planets orbiting other stars.

Today new telescopes have opened new "windows" on the universe. What will they "see" through these "windows"? What will they learn about the birth and death of stars? No astronomer can even guess. After all, they say, when the Wright brothers invented the airplane, they never dreamed of space flights to the moon or Mars.

Seven

What the Stars Have to Tell Us

Astronomers study our star and all other stars in the universe. But how does studying stars millions of miles out in space help us here on planet earth? In many ways, scientists say.

Years ago scientists asked: What makes stars shine? To answer this question, they began learning about nuclear power, the power that makes the sun give off heat and light. This process is known as fusion, the merger of two or more atoms with the subsequent release of energy.

It is not yet possible to produce energy by fusion, but today fission—or the splitting of atoms—is used in many places, which have nuclear power plants. These plants make electricity for homes and buildings. Someday nuclear power may provide fuel for our spaceships—it is already providing power for instruments on the moon and aboard satellites. This fuel—a few pounds may be all that is necessary—will power a spaceship over the great distances between planets. All this from a simple question: What makes stars shine?

Today sun power is heating homes and buildings in many towns and cities. In Maryland one man pipes water to the top of his home. The water runs down the metal roof. The sun heats the water. Collected in a tank, the hot water gives off enough heat to warm the man's home at night.

In Philadelphia a new hospital is using a system much like this to heat its many floors. So do a science museum in Virginia and a hotel in Nevada. A junior high school in Minnesota heats a large swimming pool with just three sun panels.

In New York City a new telephone company building has 170 heat-collecting panels on its roof.

So far these panels are just in the trial stage. They produce some of the heat these homes and buildings need and most of the hot water. It will take many years before we can use the sun's power to heat and light our homes and buildings as easily as gas, coal, and oil do now. But many kinds of experiments are now going on to use sun power in place of these fuels.

In Minnesota one company is working on a plan to heat 40,000 homes by sun power. It will place 74,000 mirrors on a square mile of farmland. Each mirror will be ten feet high and twenty feet wide.

Each day, as the sun moves across the sky, the mirrors will turn and follow it. They will reflect the sun's rays to a water tank. The tank will stand on top of a 1,500-foot-high tower a half mile away. A tower of power, scientists at the company call it.

The sun's rays will heat water in the tank to 1,000 degrees Fahrenheit. This hot water will turn the wheels of a huge machine that makes electricity. The electricity will be sent over power lines to homes.

Sun house. The sun heats steel plates behind the glass panels in this sun house in Minnesota. Water pumped to the roof trickles down the hot plates. The hot water flows through pipes to three 300-gallon tanks in the basement. Fans blow air over the tanks. The warm air heats the house. The tanks hold enough hot water to heat the house for three days in cloudy weather. Electric heat turns on if the house gets too cold. This house is an experiment and will go through many changes before it can be heated entirely by the sun. In years to come, houses all over America may be heated by sun power.

ROBERT KRASKE

Sun heat for schools. On the roof of this school in Maryland, 180 solar panels collect the sun's rays to heat water trickling through the panels. The heated water flows—at 156° F.—to a storage tank. From these tanks the water is pumped to classrooms, where it heats the air. The water then returns to the solar panels for reheating.

Middle Eastern governments hope to bring electricity to many small villages. How? By using sun power in solar cells. A solar cell is a wonder of modern science. It is made from crystals of silicon. Silicon is found in common sand. Removed from the sand and mixed with other chemicals, it can be formed into thin buttons. When sunshine touches these buttons, they produce

Sun carts. These small carts run on electricity from batteries. When the batteries run down, they are recharged from a bank of solar panels, which change the sun's light into electricity. The carts are, left to right, a leaf and trash remover, a small lawn mower, and a driver-operated lawn mower. Some day, battery-powered cars—their electricity generated by solar panels—may replace many gasoline-powered cars of today.

ENERGY RESEARCH AND DEVELOPMENT ADMINISTRATION

electrical current. Solar cells power the instruments on our spacecraft orbiting earth and Mars.

The day may come, scientists say, when solar cells will be tacked onto the roofs of our homes like shingles. The cells will be plugged into a wire. Each home will be its own power station. No longer will we have to depend on power coming over wires to our homes.

At the Massachusetts Institute of Technology a scientist has built an Alcator, a machine that heats hydrogen to superhot temperatures. The Alcator will give off enormous amounts of energy just the way our star does.

Moving mirrors. A close-up drawing of mirrors that could follow the sun through the day and direct its rays to a power tower. Three to four thousand mirrors like these around a tower could generate enough heat to change water into steam, which in turn could power generators to make electricity.

Power tower. An artist's drawing of one way sunlight can be changed into electricity. Mirrors on the ground follow the sun across the sky. They reflect heat to a boiler at the top of a tower. Water in the tower changes to steam. The steam is pumped to a generator in the base of the tower and turns wheels in the generator, which make electricity. A power tower like this could produce electricity for 5,000 homes.

Where will all the hydrogen come from to use in the machine? From ordinary water. Water is a liquid. In gas form, however, it is two parts hydrogen to one part oxygen. (You may have heard of H_2O.) The hydrogen in one glass of water would provide the same energy as 100 gallons of gasoline. Two glasses of water would run most cars from Washington, D.C., to San Francisco, California. Our star taught the scientist how sun power works. His machine will do what the sun does, but here on earth, not out in space.

Sun power will also make it possible to build colonies in space. Some scientists say that before the year 2050, people will live in these colonies orbiting earth.

The first colony will be in the shape of a hollow tube, or cylinder, four miles wide and nineteen miles long. It will hold up to 100,000 people.

Inside the cylinder, people will live in houses. They will grow vegetables and fruit trees. Where will they get the soil in which to plant vegetables and fruit trees? From the moon! They will fish in sparkling streams and row boats on small lakes. On the outside walls will be giant aluminum mirrors. These mirrors will reflect sunlight into the colony through blue glass. Clouds will float near the glass "sky," and light rain will fall.

Once the space colony is finished, the settlers will build huge power plants. These plants will be apart from the colony about 22,300 miles above the earth. Solar cells in giant "wings," six miles wide and seven miles across, will gather sunlight. The power plant will change the sunlight to electrical waves. It will then beam the waves to a five-mile-wide antenna on earth. Here the waves will be changed to ordinary electricity and sent over power lines to our homes and buildings. One antenna on earth could provide about half the electricity used by New York City.

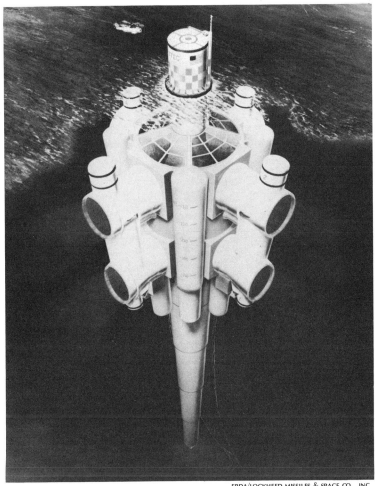

Sun power from the ocean. The upper layers of ocean water, heated by the sun, are warmer than the deeper layers—30° to 35° warmer near the equator. This temperature difference changes liquids like ammonia or propane to gas, which would turn the wheels of a generator to produce electricity. A crew living in the round checker-board tank above the water would take care of the generators and pumps. The tube runs 1,600 feet into cold water. By using sun power, this system could supply electrical power for a city of 100,000 people.

Colony in space—outside. In the next century, people from earth may live in a colony in space like this. Two long tubes, or cylinders, make up the colony. They could hold a few million people. The sun would provide power to the stations at the end of each cylinder. The "teacups" in the ring around the cylinders hold farms to grow food. Long, flat mirrors along the sides reflect sunlight into the cylinders. At left, earth and moon float in space about 200,000 miles away.

Colony in space—inside. Two cities in a space colony face each other across a broad bay. The cities are built in a cylinder 19 miles long and 4 miles wide. Sunlight would provide electricity so the colony would have power. Long flat mirrors (at the top of the picture) reflect sunlight into the colony. When the mirrors turn away from the sun, night would come—as it has to the city across the bay. In this drawing, a stream flows downhill toward the bay. A bridge, much like the golden Gate Bridge in California, joins the two cities. The city at right is in bright sunshine.

NASA

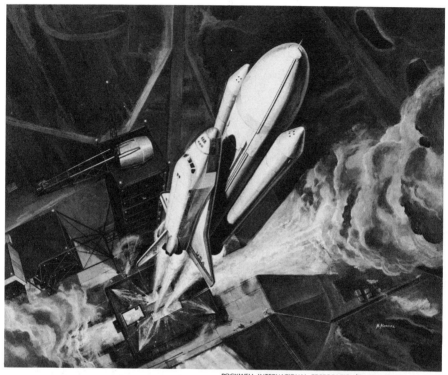

Space shuttle. In clouds of smoke and flame, the space shuttle lifts off from earth. It rides piggyback on a giant rocket. The rocket will drop off and the shuttle will continue on into space. It will deliver workers and materials to build space colonies. After delivering the materials, it will return to earth for another load. The space shuttle was to begin space flights about 1979. Space stations will be built many years after that.

Space power station. This power station will be fixed in space 22,000 miles over the United States. It will change sunlight to electrical power, which will be beamed to a power plant on earth. From the power plant, the electricity will move over lines to homes and buildings. The space shuttle at left brings workers and materials to build the space station. Workers live and work in the huge cylinders. The solar panels at the top of the picture capture sunlight and form the roof of the structure.

With sun power available night and day, our worry about the "energy crisis"—our supplies of natural gas, oil, and coal that are growing smaller—will at last be over.

What's more, there will be no air pollution or problems of running out of this clean, dependable power for all humankind. It's time to switch on the sun, scientists say. The sun is indeed our lucky star.

The stars are also teaching scientists about gravity, that mysterious force that controls the stars and planets in their paths through space.

What would happen if we could understand gravity and make it work for us?

Scientists say we might have our own sky cars. With the flick of a switch to "turn off" gravity, we could lift off the ground and float in the air. We might strap antigravity rockets on our backs and rise from the street to the top floors of tall buildings. We might even have homes in the sky. How would you like to go to Florida for the winter or maybe to the north woods of Canada for the summer? Easy! You could fly your home to wherever you wanted to go.

As for travel between planets, spaceships powered by antigravity engines could zip along at fantastic speeds. They might take only a second to travel thousands of miles. Some scientists say we may have antigravity machines before the year 2050.

Does all this sound preposterous, fantastic, unbelievable? It does to us now. But only 100 years ago, people said that airplanes, cars, TV, and space travel were "preposterous, fantastic, unbelievable."

Studying the stars will help us find the answer to a great mystery: Is there life on other planets in space?

Even with our most powerful telescopes, we can't see planets outside our solar system. We see Mars and Venus and other planets *within* our solar system. Our star shines on them just as it shines on earth and lights them up in the darkness of space. But the planets of other stars are too far away and too small for today's telescopes to find.

Scientists believe, however, that families of planets like ours may be common in the universe. Do intelligent beings live on some of these planets? Or are we alone in the universe?

People have asked these questions for many years. Two hundred years before Columbus discovered America, a Chinese named Teng Mu wrote: "How unreasonable it would be to suppose that, besides the earth and the sky which we can see, there are no other skies and no other earths!"

Today more than one scientist has said much the same thing: There is no question that we live in a universe that has thousands, maybe millions, of earthlike planets. These planets could support intelligent life. The question is not *if* but *where!*

Studying the stars helps scientists learn where intelligent life might exist. All life depends on sun power. It needs certain conditions to begin and grow.

• A planet that is not too far away or too close to a star. Too close would mean that a planet would be too hot to support life. Too far away would make a planet too cold to support life. Our earth is right in the middle of our star's "life zone."

• A star must shine steadily. Life takes 1 or 2 billion years to develop. Some large hot stars burn up their fuel in only a few million years. Some small stars burn for billions of years, but their "life zones" are too narrow.

It's unlikely that a planet would be in exactly the right place. Our star has given off an even temperature for 5 billion years—enough time for life to start and develop on our planet. It also has enough fuel for 5 billion more years.

• The temperature of a planet must stay within a narrow range. Life needs water, and the water must stay in liquid form. Too high a temperature would boil away all water. Too low a temperature and the water would change to ice.

How life develops and grows is, of course, far more complicated. It is more than the temperature and the life span and location of a planet. But from what scientists have learned so far about how life developed on earth, many believe that the same conditions could exist on other planets. Thus, life could start elsewhere in the universe.

How many planets?

In 1961 a group of scientists met at Green Bank, West Virginia. They talked about the possibility of life on other planets. They answered the question this way:

In the Milky Way—the "island," or galaxy, of 200 billion stars of which the sun and its family of planets are a part—our best guess is that there are somewhere between 40 planets and 50 million planets that could support intelligent life.

Finding what stars can support life will help astronomers know where to look for planets on which intelligent beings might live.

The wonders of the universe continue to unfold for scientists who study the stars.

Astronomers today believe they can look back in time to the beginning of the universe. The Bible says: "In the beginning . . . God said, Let there be light: and there was light." And that very probably was just how the universe was born 20 *billion* years ago.

In 1913 an American astronomer, Vesto Melvin Slipher, made an astonishing discovery. All the galaxies in the universe were moving away from each other. The Milky Way, for example, is churning through space at 1.3 million miles per hour. Imagine a balloon speckled with black dots. As the balloon blows up, the dots become farther and farther apart. The same thing is happening in the universe. Ten billion galaxies, each a space island of a billion or so stars, are speeding away from one another at fantastic speeds. The universe, Slipher found out, was expanding, growing larger and larger every second.

Well, said scientists, if this is true, if all the galaxies in the universe are flying away from one another, there must have been a time when they were all together in one large lump. By calculating the speed at which galaxies were moving apart and the distance they had traveled, scientists were able to say when the galaxies were packed together: 20 billion years ago.

But what happened way back then? What started the flight of the galaxies through the universe? An explosion, scientists say, a stupendous blast beyond anything we can imagine. The universe was born in a fireball that filled the void—the emptiness of space—with light. It was the moment of creation, the moment when time began. Scientists call it the Big Bang.

Remarkably, it's still possible, 20 billion years later, to hear the Big Bang. In 1965 scientists using radio telescopes heard a faint hiss. The hiss was radio waves. The waves were coming from all parts of the heavens and falling like gentle rain everywhere on earth. Study showed this faint hissing to be the afterglow of the Big

Bang, the echo of the moment when the cosmos—the universe—was created.

What set off the Big Bang? What caused the explosion that brought the universe into being?

"The door to the past is closed," said one scientist. "The beginning of the world is the product of some . . . event that we cannot discover. We only know that it happened."

Many scientists believe that a superior intelligence was active at the time the universe was born. "Something deeply hidden had to be behind things," Albert Einstein once said. Einstein was perhaps the most famous scientist since Isaac Newton. His work helped other scientists understand how stars are born and die.

Another scientist who marveled at the order and harmony in the universe was Sir James Jeans. "The more I contemplate the Universe," he said, "the more it seems like a great thought." Newton himself said, "This most beautiful system . . . could only proceed from an intelligent and powerful being."

Will the universe continue to expand? Some scientists think it will. Most others, though, say the time is coming when the expansion will stop.

In 1974 Allan Sandage, an astronomer in California, reported the results of a special study. The universe, he said, was expanding less rapidly than it had in the past. Gravity was tugging at the galaxies, gradually making them slow down in their outward flight. At some time in the future the expansion will stop. What then?

For a moment the galaxies will hang at rest in space. Then gravity will begin to pull, reeling in all the galaxies in the heavens. Slowly, then faster and faster, they will fly back along the path of their outward flight to the place where the Big Bang took place.

In time, in billions of years, their gases will mix.

Temperatures will rise. Perhaps there will be titanic collisions as masses of stars, thick as sand grains in a dust storm, mash together. And then what? Complete destruction? A second Big Bang? The creation of another universe?

No one knows, of course. But these are things that scientists who study the birth and death of stars have begun to think about.

Understanding the life cycle of stars, from birth to death, will help people living on earth 5 billion years from now. They will be the ones to see the first death signs of our star burning out. They will know then that the time has come—for all men and women, for all boys and girls, for birds and fish and animals, in all countries and on all islands—to leave earth for another planet. They will know that with our star dying, no life can continue on earth.

Stars die so that other stars may be born. Dying stars fling into the universe the materials from which they are made. From these materials new stars and new planets are created—and live and die. The earth and sun and all people on earth are made up, in good part, from the materials in dying stars. Said one scientist: "Except for hydrogen, everything in our bodies has been produced in the thermonuclear reactions in stars." As much as people are children of earth, we are also children of the stars. Earth is only our temporary home, and in the stars lies our future.

Understanding the stars means understanding the great universe in which we live and of which we are a tiny but important part. Like a single wheel in a great clock, we turn with all other "wheels" in the universe. The whole clock is part of us, and we are part of the whole clock.

Scientists say, too, that we don't know yet what we will learn from understanding how stars are born and how they die. We have only the smallest hint of the wonders that stars have to teach us. What we have learned so far, amazing as it is, is only the beginning. More astonishing wonders are yet to come. The truth about the stars and how they live and die is beyond our present imagination.

You must recognize, said one astronomer, that we are just beginning to learn about the universe. Many surprises, even the most extraordinary surprises, are possible.

Index